The Seven Steps to Career Consciousness

Get the job you deserve.

by
Louise Lapish

Published by The Solopreneur Publishing Company Ltd,
Unit 4, Cedars Business Centre, Barnsley Road, Hemsworth, Pontefract, West Yorkshire WF9 4PU.
www.thesolopreneur.co.uk

The Solopreneur (Publishing Company) Ltd focuses on the needs of each individual author client. This book has been published through their 'Solopreneur Self-Publishing (SSP)' brand that enables authors to have complete control over their finished book whilst utilising the expert advice and services usually reserved for traditionally published print, in order to produce an attractive, engaging, quality product. Please note, however, that final editorial decisions and approval rested with the author. The publisher takes no responsibility for the accuracy of the content.

ISBN 978-0-9930569-7-0

Printed in the U.K. by Charlesworth Press, Wakefield, West Yorkshire.

PREFACE

When I grow up I want to be...

Thank you to my amazing family and friends who have helped me with this book and supported me throughout the writing process and the many years leading up to it. Special thanks to everyone who has encouraged me and of course, all the clients and colleagues who have been on this journey with me.

A note to Alex and Sophie.....always believe you can be whatever your heart tells you.

If you'd have asked me as a child what I wanted to be when I grew up, the answers would vary from being a hedgehog to becoming a writer. I guess I made the writer part come true by the fact you're reading this book. It wasn't a simple process; there were hundreds of poems, blogs and articles to get me to this point and it was still a slow transition from the fountain pen to the keyboard. Yet here we are.

So, why do I talk about 'career consciousness'? Believe it or not, taking charge of your career and job search is all in your head. I've never doubted that the people I've coached and supported over the years could achieve whatever it was they wanted to achieve. Some would call it blind faith, others believe that the power of the mind can make anything possible. I am happy in the middle ground. I have had the privilege of helping hundreds of people achieve their career goals, and I have always maintained belief in their goal, even when they may have doubted themselves. Clients often state that my positivity was the one constant throughout the rollercoaster ride towards being career conscious.

My positive state was one element; the other key thing was objectivity. It's very difficult when you're in a tough situation to see a way out of it. The mortgage still needs to be paid, you need food on the table, and so on. Yet life is too short to be in a job you dislike, spending hours and hours clock-watching. I wanted to put together a simple and straightforward guide to help you take control of your career. These steps do work, and I've seen them enable people to achieve their desired outcomes time and time again. My message is simple: it's never just about securing your elusive next role – it's about planning and shaping your career until the day you retire. It's your choice. You will not use this book once, but every two to three years to ensure you remain in control every step of the way.

I have seen people achieve things they thought were impossible, which only strengthened my resolve with the next client; I knew that they could achieve anything they wanted, and so can you. Now are you ready to become career conscious?

How to use this book....

Warning: This book is not an easy read. I expect you to work hard; you may need to challenge yourself, and in some cases, reprogram your grey matter. It's intended to be a workbook and step by step guide to support you through your job search or complete career change. Grab a notebook or pad and be prepared to work through the different exercises; then gain an understanding as to how you can communicate that verbally and in writing, as well as convince the employer that you're the best person for the job. It's about raising your awareness of the rules and tools of the job search and empowering you to use them.

Are you ready?

Step One: Own up to being a grown-up
Let's start at the very beginning: what do you want to do?

Step Two: Location, vocation, frustration
Shape the dream, visualise your perfect environment and create your job checklist

Step Three: Sell your 'tell'
Once upon a time there was a happy ending; understand how to tell your story with passion and impact.

Step Four: Application Sensation
Create winning documents to dazzle your audience

Step Five: Let's talk the talk
Develop your killer interview techniques

Step Six: Recruiters, rejection and networking
Plan and execute a proactive job search

Step Seven: Be kind to your mind
Keeping positive, productive and proactive

Step One: Own up to being a grown-up

Let me ask you a question: have you ever wondered how you ended up in your current job or career? I suppose the fact that you're reading this book, and have made a decision to take control of your career, suggests the answer is 'yes'. Together, we're going to work on seven simple steps so that you're ready to make the career changes you want, and need to, make.

Let's take you on a journey to your younger days. What was your dream career then? A doctor, a fire-fighter, or something more magical? Is the job you have today the one you dreamt of; does it meet all the expectations you had? The truth is that, when we are children, very few of us know what type of job we want to do - we don't really know what types of role exist in the big, wide world. Think of all the changes that have happened in your lifetime; new jobs emerge every day, as both the world and technology moves on, and old jobs disappear into the ether. Long gone are the 'knocker-uppers', whose responsibilities involved walking the streets of the mill towns, knocking on windows to ensure factory workers arrived promptly at work.

A few people I know followed their childhood ambitions; a friend of mine was born to be a doctor, and now she is a highly revered consultant in geriatric care. Throughout school she took the right courses and completed the right amount of work, coupled with her natural intelligence it was a sure-fire recipe for success. When one of her siblings came to me to talk about her career and was considering a career change, it was obvious how growing up next to someone so steadfast could prove difficult, especially if you, like most of us, have no fixed idea about what you want to do.

Another client told me about her son, Sam; the first time he ever went on holiday he was fascinated by the luggage carousel. He decided at that very moment he wanted to be a baggage handler. Fourteen years later he landed his dream job, and he still loves going to work every day. Sam's mother said she never believed he would do it, but she was very glad he proved her wrong. If we're honest, though, not everyone is as lucky as Sam or Dr Hannah.

Not knowing what you want to do is normal

Now that we've acknowledged that, we can move on. Did you receive any career advice at school? If it was anything like mine it was a number of tick-box exercises, with little or no sophistication. Would you prefer to work indoors or outdoors? As a young teen the thought of manual labour, working outdoors, seemed a million miles away from my world. Can you remember what your results were? My results came back with suggestions like 'librarian' and 'teacher'. I remember even then being bemused by the nature of the questions. If they'd asked me whether having books in the right alphabetical order was of the slightest importance, the answer would have been a resounding 'no'! Surely this would have to be a prerequisite if you're going to be a librarian? What about teaching? As children seem to sense my fear (my gorgeous godson, Alex, and his sister, Sophie, excluded), I'm not sure it would have been the right environment for me. In fact, being stuck in school forever would have been a fate worse than death.

Fascinated by the quest to find out what makes some people follow their dreams and others to settle, prompted me to ask the question to Yorkshire Mafia members (one of Yorkshire's largest and most active business communities). Some of the responses were fantastic, illustrating the diverse, and somewhat obscure.

Traditional job or creative endeavours?

'I've been told (many times in the pub) that at the age of five, I was asked what I wanted to be. I answered, 'I want to be a solicitor so I can sit in a big chair'. No idea where that came from. I've got a big chair, though'. **Adrian W**

NB. Adrian now works as a commercial photographer. A little different to the world of law.

'I had a different grown-up aspiration every week when I was little; lawyer, speech therapist, vet, artist, prime minister! I think I always believed that I would just find I was marvellous at one thing and that would seal the deal, but as I grew up I discovered I was more of an all-rounder, meaning I had to find a future career rather than it finding me.

My first attempt appeared to be a false start, a fine art degree seemed to lead nowhere, and I then went on to join a business at a level that did not require a graduate, never mind a knowledge of art. I joined the world of procurement at assistant level, enjoyed it, and before long, ten years had gone by and I was a senior manager. As I've matured I have found a renewed pleasure in creativity, and now separate my time between the two, working as a procurement consultant by day and producing artwork and illustration by night. My artwork is appearing in a book this month, which is very exciting! We all live so long these days and retirement age is being pushed back further and further, it's no surprise that people can have two or three careers in their lifetime and be accomplished at all of them. Perhaps, after asking our children what they want to be, we should follow this up with another question: 'and then what?' **Victoria W**

'I wanted to be a film director when I was a little girl. I also wanted to be an actress, as I was in all the school plays and very dramatic. As a teenager I lost confidence and direction, so didn't follow the dream through....yet. My dream is still alive. As well as my day job, I also do a lot of writing and have recently been published in an anthology of Leeds' writers' flash fiction, describing a short film I want to make. The door is still open! In the meantime, I'm a business development manager and I do a lot of events involving planning and coordinating – 'pretend directing' in a funny kind of way!' **Aissa G**

'When I was young, I thought I'd end up as a professional musician. I'm now a professional fundraiser and a keen amateur/semi-pro musician. I also quite fancied being an interpreter at one point. Music is your friend for life - paid or unpaid.' **Helen M**

Is it really a man's world? Not for these ladies.

'I was ridiculed and bullied for being in the woodwork class at school - the only girl amongst 63 pupils (back in 1976/7). Only three managed to achieve O Level grade, of which I was one. I was laughed at again in cabinet making and wood machining, the only girl on the course, and one of only two in that year group to receive a distinction in Advanced Cabinet Making and Furniture Design. That showed them. Mum and Dad were proud; Dad had been in the building trade all his life. Girls/ladies: never be put off because it's a male dominated environment. I spend most of my time now on building sites, in charge of men. I'm still waiting for the elusive female joiner/electrician/ plumber/ site manager, etc.; I'm sure there must be some, somewhere.' **Jacqueline C**

'I wanted to be a doctor, then an actress, and finally an RAF navigator. My careers teacher informed me that 'working class girls with comprehensive school educations do not become RAF aircrew', and, if I worked hard and got my predicted As and Bs, I could be a nurse or a teacher. My dad went mental when I got home and stormed into the school, asking if they'd recruited the careers teacher from the 1950s. I did end up becoming a navigator in the RAF after all, but I don't know if I'd have been as determined if that careers advisor hadn't been so sexist/classist/whateverist. She probably did me a favour!' **Charley D**

Dreaming about flying above the clouds and further afield

'I wanted to be an airline pilot. I failed maths O Level three times on the trot, realised that goal was a little out of reach for me and ended up with a hang-gliding licence and a job as a translator. I like the outdoors, a bit of adrenaline from time to time, and am a Europhile. There's some logic there, but as it turned out, not much career planning; I'm still waiting for an honorary degree from somewhere. That would be handy because I'd like to now be a German teacher, but not one tied to the National Curriculum.' **Jim M**

'Aged eight: I wanted to work for NASA, designing and building space shuttles. It wasn't much more than a childhood fantasy; I've never been enough of a mathematician for serious engineering work! Aged fifteen: I wanted to join military intelligence, either the Army or RAF, as a commissioned officer. Asthma put paid to that one. Aged twenty: I wanted to go into academia, and follow up my degrees with a PhD, then work in policy-linked academia around international security, diplomacy and development. That was a case of 'close, but no cigar' on the PhD studentship funding, at least once a year over six annual application rounds. I'd still like to give that a go if I ever find the money to fund the PhD myself.' **David H-C**

'I wanted to be an astronaut, and it wasn't just a passing fancy, as I applied again to the NASA programme a couple of decades back. After successive governments dismantled our manned mission programme I aimed to be an RAF pilot and fancied transport over combat; my eyesight got in the way of that, though. Third choice was a scientist, and I did become a physicist for a while. I've done quite a few things over the years, all with some technical or scientific basis, leading to running my own business, which I set up almost five years ago.' **Simon H**

'I wanted to be a jet fighter pilot. When I went to the RAF to join up at the age of eighteen, they didn't allow women to do that job. Funnily enough, I mentioned yesterday that I felt entirely happy and free with what I am doing now: running my own business and loving it. I'm on the front line, working with businesses on sales, and in my personal life, I've got my CBT tomorrow to get my full bike licence, which I reckon takes just about the same wits and attention needed to fly a jet'. **Chrissie S**

Doctor, doctor.....

'I wanted to be a doctor, and even did science A Levels, but I did not have the brains to get the grades. So, I decided to study psychology, and here I am, a chartered psychologist and loving what I do. I may have shot for the stars and landed on the moon but it isn't that bad going and I have (mostly) no regrets. My main regret is not having the brains to finish a Ph.D.; I'm still hankering after the title 'Doctor'!' **Ian F**

And now for something completely different...

'I was another who wanted to be a bin man...no idea why, I just did. I never followed that path but went into IT and have been there ever since (except for 18 months doing project management). But I still haven't decided what I want to do when I grow up.' **Martin W**

'Well, I never wanted to be a pilot - I wanted to be a vet. Because I had focus, the advice I was given was what to do next. I did the GCSEs, worked on farms, got A Levels, couldn't get motivated, and lost focus. Was all that effort wasted? Regrets? No! It was still great experience.' **Toby T**

'Having watched Dirty Dancing hundreds of times, I decided I wanted to be a holiday camp dancer (I still do).' **Chris H**

I received hundreds of stories from my contacts, some admitting they just wanting to marry someone famous; several dreamt of being professional footballers, budding thespians, female mechanics, a few longed to be superheroes, and many that told stories about being held back by teachers, parents, and most definitely themselves. The one resounding theme that came through is that it was never too late to do something different; changing career is becoming normal (more on that later). It's time to think about what's stopping you making the changes you want to make. What is holding you back?

Own up to being a grown-up

As many of my contacts stated, they do not want to grow up and simply get older, either gracefully or disgracefully. The key thing to remember is that you have absolute control over what you do with your life; even if you feel that the change happening at the moment was forced upon you. In a few moments I'm going to ask you to really start to take control and become career conscious.

Why did you choose your current path? Very few people have the luxury of being 100% conscious when they make career choices. If you consider the aforementioned career stories it becomes clear that few people have a calling, a vocation or an actual plan. Most of the stories highlighted that people fell into their first couple of roles; they were not conscious of their career choices, decisions were often based on income - working with friends, joining the family business, and so on. How many of these people forgot or postponed their education once they had the comfort of regular money in their pocket? If you find yourself being a 'one day' or a 'someday' kind of a person now is the time to stop and make the changes you want to make.

I have asked hundreds of my career coaching clients over the years why they chose a particular path. I received various answers but many said: 'my dad, uncle, cousin was a ......; my parents said.......; I fell in to it, and stayed there for.......' Do any of these sound familiar? When we begin our careers, our world can appear quite small, our experiences, limited, and often, they're based on the people we come in contact with. How often have you heard the phrase 'he/she followed in their father's footsteps'?

Many of the career change clients I have worked with in their thirties, forties and fifties have had long and successful careers, but have never felt that their role was the right one. Lawyers, accountants and other professionals are some of the most common career change candidates. Situations, jobs and people change; what seemed like a good fit initially won't always stay that way. At some point there's a trigger, and they decide they need to be happy and satisfied in their working week; they need to banish that Monday morning feeling and make a positive change.

As we are all expected to work longer, having more than one distinct career in your life is becoming increasingly common. The concept of the job for life has all but disappeared. My dad served in the police force for thirty years - people changing jobs and career is an alien concept to him. People are often worried about being seen as a job hopper; yet perhaps this is better than being institutionalised. Staying at one company can be as damaging as changing roles.

Take a moment to think about all the jobs that didn't exist when you were at school or college. We would never have heard of people talking about being a social media guru or mobile app developer (though I'm sure many of us hoped being cabin crew in outer space would now be reality). The key to remaining career conscious is to realise that things will never stay the same. This doesn't mean hopping from company to company like a butterfly, it's simply ensuring that you avoid being stuck in a rut and you're instead planning your next move.

It is startling that, in general, people spend less time thinking about and planning their careers than they do their annual holiday. Would you leave any other part of your life to chance in the same way? Some countries embrace professional career services, and individuals are regularly coached to drive their happiness and success. In my experience, career planning and people development are fairly new concepts to most people in the UK. Many feel like they should already have the answers. If your car breaks down you'd contact a mechanic - why would seeking specialist advice on your career be any different? The exercises in this book will help you to be your own coach. Ready?

Exercise One: Own up to being a grown-up

The time has come - own up to being a grown-up and get ready to take control. Grab your notebook and take your time to work through the following questions.

1. Think back to your childhood. Write down all the jobs you remember wanting as a child or teenager.
2. Now, taking each of those jobs in turn, consider what it was that appealed to you about these roles?
3. What aspects of the role do you think you would have relished?
4. Did you ever try any of them, and if so, what did you enjoy?
5. Are there any similarities between your dream job and your current or last role?
6. What made you choose your first ever job? How did that work out for you?
7. What made you choose the second job? (You may choose to run through each of the roles you have had, to look for recurring patterns)
8. What attracted you to your current/last position?
9. What elements in the past have prevented you from taking action? What has held you back?
10. On a scale of 1- 10 how career conscious (in control) have you felt throughout your career?
11. On a scale of 1- 10 how in control would you like to be in your next move?

Summary of Step One
Are you ready to take control?

Remember:

Not knowing what you want to do is normal! So is having more than one career.

Own up to being a grown-up and accept that you have the power to change your current position.

Make a list of all the positive things that will help you become more career conscious.

Step Two: Location, vocation, frustration

In this chapter it's time for you to get down to the nitty gritty; you need to shape your personal goals and prepare a checklist. You're on your way towards being career conscious and choosing the right next step for you. Remember, your ideal position may be a step or two away; it's okay to plan your next couple of steps, or even three - as long as you have a plan you can achieve it.

What did you learn from exercise one about your choices to date? Were you conscious in your decision-making? The English dictionary definition of the word 'career' is: a *chosen pursuit or occupation or, if we are to use it as a verb: to move swiftly along; rush in an uncontrolled way.* Which of these definitions is the most fitting for your career to date?

What about the definition of consciousness? *'The mental activity of which a person is aware as contrasted with unconscious mental processes.'* You're stepping away from unconscious career choices and becoming increasingly aware of how you can make desired changes.

Do you consider that you made a choice, or was it a series of incidents that set you on the path you're on today? Did you leave school or university, take the first position you were offered, then work your way up through the hierarchy? Or the alternative: trying a few different roles until you found one that felt like a good fit? Neither of these are incorrect, especially if they were the only options you were aware of at the time.

I spoke to a client recently who said that in his early career the only enjoyment he used to get at work was trying not to do any work – he was left unchallenged, bored and frustrated. Another lady I came into contact with absolutely loathed her role, the organisation and her boss; this was more than apparent to those unlucky enough to work for her. She was counting down the days until her retirement, a sad state for someone twenty years away from that stage of her life. Her life was one of constant stress and misery. It seemed more likely either her physical or mental health would fail before she reached her elusive goal - a clear example of someone who felt stuck in a rut and not career conscious.

This doesn't just happen at the early stages. How many people do you know who have wondered if this is it for their career? Cycles are perfectly normal in all aspects of our lives. The more people get used to adapting and changing, the more conscious employers will become, and realise that it's not just possible but, importantly, good for business. Both the third and public sector have found themselves fishing in the private sector pool for expertise and vice versa. They've all identified the need for a broad spectrum of people and talent. Remember, changing roles within your organisation can be as valuable as looking in the open market.

The next step to career consciousness

I recently coached a client, Robert, who worked in insurance. He desperately wanted to move out of the sector, he certainly never dreamt as a child that he would spend his days discussing renewals or working to make a large organisation more money. What did he dream of? Perhaps being a footballer or an entertainer. Someone at some point in his life told him these things were not possible. Insurance paid the bills but didn't inspire him; in fact, it made him miserable. He enjoyed working with the people around him, and every once in a while a project would spark his interest and re-engage him, or the suggestion he was in line for a promotion kept him chained. It needed something bigger to spark the fuse for change!

When people are faced with redundancy or a major life-changing event, they often tell me they want to do something that matters, to give something back to the world. This is not always realistic when it comes to the financial implications, but it's by no means impossible. The first thing to check is their commitment to that goal. It may simply mean a series of stepping stones towards their ultimate goal. People wanting to test the third sector often volunteer alongside their day job, providing invaluable exposure to the environment. Consciousness is not about rose-tinted glasses. Now back to Robert making major changes as the countdown to a big birthday began (the spark that lit his fuse). Through several one to one sessions we picked away at what he did and didn't want to do. Where did he feel he would fit in? What were his passions? One thing that became really clear was that his rut extended to more than his job. He wanted to buy a house but didn't know where he wanted to live, he felt love was escaping him too. Everything was making him miserable. Do you ever have days like that? To say that we spend so little time planning our careers, they really do have a major impact on every area of our lives.

Industry insanity - size really does matter

One of the initial things that became obvious to Robert was that he was dissatisfied with the industry; he did not like what insurance was becoming, he was not driven by profit, and he cared about the impact his work had on the world. It's common for people to rule out certain industries, such as tobacco, arms, chemicals, to name a few. He was increasingly discontent with the size and the culture of the organisation; he needed to be able to make a difference, and in an enormous company he found this difficult. What did he learn through this process? He identified the size of the organisation he wanted to work for, he knew he wanted to be a bigger fish in a smaller pond. Remember, often knowing what you don't want can be as important as being clear about what you do want! For example, what kind of organisation, and how large a company, would it need to be, to allow you to stand out in the way you would like to?

Company culture vulture

It's not uncommon for people to stay working for a manager they detest, or in a role that frustrates them, simply because of the positive relationship with their colleagues. They get on with the people they work with and fear they may not find that same friendship in a new role. On the flip side, office politics, game playing and back-stabbing are often terms synonymous with the world of work. Are you a culture vulture – do you know what environment makes you thrive and which would send you running for the hills? Most of us have worked for a manager or team leader we didn't like; they run on negatives rather than positives. They can range between extremes of micro management or complete abandonment. A trip to the coffee machine is usually coupled with gossip from bitter and de-motivated colleagues. What culture would ensure you thrive? After some volunteer work Robert knew that he wanted to work in the charity sector, yet still utilise his many years of commercial experience.

Take a moment to think about your fit with your team - do you respect them? Do you get on with them? Not getting on with team members or a boss is one of the leading reasons why people leave a role. How would you like those future relationships to be? What are you looking for in a boss? Robert highlighted that he wanted to develop and manage people; working in insurance, his manager thought his skill set was better utilised elsewhere. This was great for the company but not so good for

Robert. He knew that in the next company, people development had to be one of their key values. Have you ever felt that you've been held back to suit business requirements?

Perhaps you're sitting there wondering how you can ever leave the sector you're in, you still have no idea who might be interested in what you have to offer, or you're not sure how you can find out if an organisation has the right culture and values for you. Remember, we're working through your plan step by step; nothing can stop you taking control and putting your plan into action.

The work-life balancing act

Being career conscious, you need to visualise what the perfect role looks like for you. This includes work-life balance. Work-life balance is far from being a myth, your career is important but remember, 'we work to live, not live to work'. During the recession many people felt that they had little or no choice; feeling lucky to even have a job, they worked harder with fewer and fewer colleagues to cover the roles. A client told me his trigger for change was the work pressure; one evening, he emailed his boss at 2am as he was working until the early hours. When he received an immediate reply he knew it was time to change. He would never meet all of their expectations.

How do we consider balance rather than the constant juggling act? What would you spend more of your free time doing if you had the right balance? On the flip side, if your current position already gives you the ideal balance, what are you prepared to sacrifice for your new job? I mentioned Robert had seen himself as unlucky in love, and he wanted to settle down and plant some roots. The fact that he had neither of these things turned into a real positive when it came to looking for new opportunities. He was free to go where ever his dream job would take him. Remember, this is your vision, there are no right or wrong answers. It's perfectly okay to want more time with family and loved ones; ensure this becomes part of your job specification, the one you're focusing on.

Occupational offerings and obstacles

I'm going to ask you to defragment your day to day role, or your last position, to understand what it really means. What does/did the role entail? Start to think about the less obvious elements to your role. For example, in Robert's case, he used a project management framework to deliver new insurance initiatives; he influenced people to ensure the projects were delivered on time, he had high levels of accuracy and attention to detail. He didn't just work in insurance, he was not simply a job title; he had a broad range of skills. What skills and strengths do you need to ensure that your day to day achievements are met? What do you have to offer a new employer? What makes you different and special? You have to make it easy for someone in a new sector or organisation to understand how your skills match their needs. One of the biggest obstacles you need to overcome is the assumption that an employer can naturally make the leap between your current role and your potential new one. You have to show them how you will sparkle in your new role.

Believe, then begin

How did this work for Robert? We carefully identified which of his strengths would match the requirements of the third sector and began to drill them down. The more we matched his skills and strengths, the more confident and conscious he became. He started to see how he could prove himself somewhere new. You will start to feel the same confidence when you decide what is it you WANT to offer. Notice I use the word WANT, if you would prefer not to use a particular skill, now is the time to ditch it. This is about you taking control. You may be the world's whizz at PowerPoint but if you never want to see another slide again, now is the time to make the choice. A potential employer only knows what you tell them. (I was once asked by an employer if I could use Excel macros...I could but it was never needed.)

I supported Clare recently who told me 'she was just a cleaner'. Clare was a cleaning supervisor of a small team of four; she had never considered her management skills, her communication skills, her stock ordering skills, and the countless other things she relied on every single day. No one is 'just' an anything, every role brings value to an organisation. Once you see it that way, and acknowledge your skills and strengths, the rest will start to fall into place.

Money, money, money, not so funny

It would be futile to suggest that remuneration was not important, and if money were no object perhaps our choices would be somewhat different. What is the ideal figure you have in mind? Have you researched the job market and analysed salary surveys – what's your overall package worth? How important is money to you, or are other elements of the package more important, i.e. pension, flexi-time, holiday days, childcare, uniform or dress code...the list is endless. Robert decided he could afford to take a small pay cut for his dream job and the chance to move into a new sector - he remained realistic about what he needed to earn. As it turned out, when that job arrived, it was almost financially equivalent to the previous one. They even helped him relocate.

Redundancy or wake-up call?

You may be reading this and thinking that's all well and good if you are choosing to make the change. What if it isn't really your choice and you simply need a job - any job? The everyday issues need to be dealt with, the mortgage needs to be paid. It's okay to take a role as income replacement, but keep conscious about your career goal. If change was forced upon you or redundancy came as a bolt out of the blue, how you choose to handle it will dictate how easily you move into a new role - the right new role. Consciousness and mindset are crucial in terms of creating opportunity. Is your glass half full or half empty? Or are you grateful there's something in the glass at all? My clients have often had difficult times at work before they were made redundant, uncertainty can cause lots of unneeded stress. Sometimes, the situation is handled badly by the organisation and this can often leave the person feeling the decision was very personal. Redundancy is a commercial decision, not a personal one. Others, like Robert, had often hoped to be made redundant so that the decision to jump was made by someone else. He ultimately realised that he had to take control and drive the change; now it's your turn.

Does your cloud have a silver lining?

It struck me that when change is happening to people it's difficult to see the silver lining of their situation. With hindsight they usually do, much later when they are in their new role and much happier. Having change forced upon a work situation can be scary and it's understandable that people are concerned their whole life will fall apart. What are we without a job title, a purpose? People will settle for second or third best, simply because they're fearful of what the change might bring. It's very easy for me, as I can look at the success stories of the hundreds of clients I've worked with; I have complete confidence that things always turn out for the best. How did you feel during the redundancy process - are you still holding on to emotional baggage from that situation? If you're holding on to any of the bitterness or misplaced loyalty then it's time to let it go and start to focus on your next goal.

What stories will you tell the younger generation?

In the following exercise I'm going to ask you to think about what you would like to be remembered for, what stories would you like to tell the younger generation? I remember complete joy from hearing my grandma tell hundreds of stories about her life. She had numerous jobs and experiences, but which were the ones she talked about the most? The ones that brought her the happiest memories, and they were all from her time in the Land Army. She talked fondly of her time in the fields of Scotland: the people she met, the challenges she faced, being squashed by various cattle, and the joy of being able to take fresh eggs to her family on home visits. The things that gave her the best memories were intangible, not the packages; she had no pension, no company car - instead, more gratitude for a solid pitchfork and strong relationships that lasted well beyond the war years.

If I think about the stories that I will tell people in the future, many of them are rooted in the successes my clients have had. Taking 'the call' from a client who has secured a fantastic new position never gets old. I really do have the best job in the world. So, what about Robert? He utilised his professional experience and successfully managed the transition process into the third sector. He utilised his ability to 'sell his tell' (more on this in step three) to prove how he could make the change and bring maximum impact. Robert is now enjoying his new international role making a real difference to the lives of many people, all because he had a plan and the right mindset. He remained 100% career conscious throughout the process.

Make sure you can see the wood for the trees

I appreciate I'm in a fortunate position; every day I hear positive job news, clients securing interviews, jobs and contracts. This type of feedback directly contravenes the news that filters through to us every day, i.e. fears of recession and job losses. Having an objective view and being like Robert - having a clear goal and taking the right type of action - generates results. When you're looking at things from your own perspective it's often difficult to see the wood for the trees. Resetting to a positive and 100% career conscious state can be the most difficult part. Rest assured you can secure the right new position; let's work out what that position looks like for you.

Exercise Two: Location, Vocation, Frustration

Time to start thinking about those choices. Ensure you're somewhere you won't be distracted, this is all about you and your future job happiness. What processes make your job work; how do you impact on the people around you?

1. Think about all the times you have had to handle change. Which emotions did you experience?
2. Take a moment to visualise the perfect

organisation for you; size, number of colleagues, location, industry, ethics, etc.

3. What stands out to you the most about this organisation?

4. How proud are you to work for your current/last organisation?

5. What would need to be the same/different in your new organisation?

6. What would you most like to be remembered for by your colleagues?

7. What would you most like to be remembered for by your boss?

8. What would you most like to be remembered for by your family?

9. What are your top 10 - 20 skills and strengths

1.	11.
2.	12.
3.	13.
4.	14.
5.	15.
6.	16.
7.	17.
8.	18.
9.	19.
10.	20.

10. Highlight which of these bring you the most pleasure and enjoyment when utilised

11. What is it you enjoy about these skills?

12. Why might these be valuable to a new employer?

13. Are there any additional skills that might make this easier?

14. How can you gain those skills?

15. Now ask a trusted colleague or relative to give you feedback on what they think your

strengths and skills are – remember, they see you differently.

16. Now create the perfect job advert for your dream job – what would it be doing, where would it be located, how much would they pay you?

Summary of Step Two

Being career conscious is a choice; know what feels right and wrong for you. Remember this is about 'WANT', and your future happiness. Keep the job you want at the forefront of your mind.

Step Three: Sell your tell

Once upon a time.....have I got your attention? Then I'll begin. Once upon a time there was a happy ending, surely that's all we need to know? Our society is built on stories, passed down from generation to generation; we loved them as children and even now many of us still get lost in a book. Take those key strengths and skills you identified in chapter two and start to think about how you're going to prove you have them to a potential employer. You are going to evaluate those skills. Who are the buyers (potential employers) who would be interested in your experience? How have you made an impact and added value to your organisation? Step three is about selling your impact and passion through powerful stories.

It's important to go through the important stage of self-reflection to identify your strengths, it's crucial that you formulate a way to talk about them and sell them to others. An interviewer will not read between the lines; and even if you think 'you were just doing your job', you need to show them how you are different to the next candidate. Candidates tend not to be employed because they're the same as the others, but on how/why they're different. If you know what you're selling and you know who might be interested in buying, your job search becomes much simpler.

Be objective about your objective

After step two, you'll be clearer about what an organisation has to offer you to make it the right choice. Think about the job advert you created, what do you need? Use your checklist as a focus, it's all too easy to lose sight of this and settle for second best. Remember this is a two-way process, they have to be able to offer you something in return.

Are you looking to escape your current position?

Remain conscious at every stage; you may feel the need to escape from your current position, and even though you might just want to get out, you know what it is you're looking for. We've all heard the idiom that you could jump from the frying pan into the fire. This often turns out to be the case; one bad day can trigger such negative emotions. To keep career conscious you need to be calm and confident. Make the changes when you're ready, no matter how challenging that may feel. Plan your escape carefully.

Did change happen around you?

Sometimes life throws you a curve ball, at first it can send you reeling in shock, and everything you thought you could rely on changes. Once the initial shock subsided did you look back and think that the warning signs were there? As humans, we're often guilty of going through life with blinkers on. The writing may be on the wall yet we choose to ignore it. This approach is also a defence mechanism; we don't want to think about the bad things that may happen. This uncertainty can make you less objective about your objective.

Curve balls are not always as bad as you thought if you change your perspective. Recently, I worked with Mark, an Operations Director; he was facing his third redundancy in five years and feeling very negative. During the defragmentation of his role, it became very clear he was exceptional at delivering positive change quickly. He was, in fact, making himself redundant. This was not a question of changing his ethos and working slower, or more ineffectively, it was about changing his perspective. He began to realise redundancy meant he had delivered what the organisation needed and he should be expecting this as part of his role. The other crucial thing he recognised was that the turbulent change element was the only part he thrived on; he didn't enjoy the status quo. For him, redundancy became a win-win; he decided short-term contracts were the way forward.

If you're not in work it's tempting to apply for every position you see - in an approach known as 'spraying and praying', sending out a CV to anybody and everybody, crossing your fingers, and hoping that someone will save you, and offer you that ideal position. All this will do is increase the amount of rejection you'll face, you'll hear the same old excuses and, even worse, take things personally. Keeping to your plan or objective will ensure you remain on track. Keep career conscious; you are in control of this job search, you only need one position.

Back to the story telling...

Preparing your career stories is time well spent, not only will it remind you of the impact you made, it will increase your confidence and ensure that you're ready for anything - including interviews. Why do you need to tell stories? Think about the land army stories; we have to find a way of making your stories memorable and your differences shine.

Candidate one: I tripled sales in year one.

Tripling sales? This sounds like an achievement he should be proud of. What questions are going through your mind? How, why, what did this mean? There's almost an element of disbelief at such a bold statement - might an interviewer think the same? Are you the type of person who finds it difficult to talk about the positive things you've done? This is a really common approach, hoping other people take the hint, read between the lines and understand your story. Even in appraisals it's common to undersell yourself. I'm not talking about boasting or exaggerating, simply demonstrating your positives.

Candidate two: I identified that there was a gap in the product line. I used market knowledge to source the required product, negotiated with the supplier and secured a significant saving, and led the product to launch. It proved very popular, tripling add-on sales and generating an extra £20,000 for the company.

Once the candidate delivered the story in a way that shows us 'how' we're much more likely to believe it. As they say in court, 'it's all about the evidence, my lord!' How can you put your strengths and skills into stories that make it easy for other people to understand you? There are some systems you can use to ensure you provide the right type of information: STAR being one of the most well-known. You may be familiar with this process if you've ever completed a competency-based interview, or even in appraisals.

S Situation
T Task
A Action
R Result

Think about the STAR steps of and utilise them as a framework for your compelling stories.

Situation and Result

Situation and Result; think about these two elements together. If you can identify your start and end point everything else is simple. How can you prove you made a positive impact on a situation? This is often one of the biggest challenges people face as they see it as being boastful or bragging. I prefer to think of telling a STAR story without a result like a joke without a punch-line. If there's no clear result or happy ending, is there any point even talking about the situation?

What does this look like? Let's use the example of candidate two.

Situation: The first part of my job is always to look at the current product range and identify if there are any gaps. If I can identify a product that our customers might need it makes the whole experience easier for them.

Result: I identified that there was a gap in the product line; it proved very popular, tripling add-on sales and generating an extra £20,000 for the company.

The result is always the happy ending. It's usually one of the recognisable heroes: saving time, saving money, making money, improving how things work, or making customers happy. All the stories we love usually have something going wrong and then a hero to put them right. In your story that hero is you!

Have a think about what you've been the most proud of so far in your current role – why might another company be interested in that story? What does that story offer them? Remember, they need to recognise why you might be the solution to a challenge they're facing. How can you prove you're their hero?

Task and Actions

When it comes to the task, the question I always ask is 'why did they choose you to complete it?' What made you special and different? The usual answer is 'because I was the only one there, or no one else could do it.' Was this really the reason? It's often more likely due to your previous experience in an area, or a previous success - perhaps it was a difficult client and you've always maintained a great relationship with them. These are the reasons you need to get used to discussing when 'selling your tell'.

This reason can link you straight to the actions. This is often the hardest bit if you're trying to describe what you do, day in and day out. To you, it's obvious, to your audience it isn't. If you have ever looked at one of your colleagues and thought, 'how do they get away with doing so little? How can they speak to customers like that? Why do they do everything the hard way?' Turn that around: what do you do differently, what makes it work better for you? Why do you find it easy?

What does it mean?

Think about your proudest achievement story - what happened, who were the important characters? How were you the hero? Work through it using the four STAR stages;

Situation   What was going wrong?
What needed to work better?
What would have happened if you hadn't fixed it?
Why were you completing the task?

Customer Service example: The customer complaints were going up, the service levels were not as good as they used to be, and repeat business was falling. There was a worry that customers would choose a competitor.

Desired result: Deliver a better service, avoid complaints, resolve current complaints and keep the customers happy. What steps might be needed to turn this situation around?

IT example: Systems were failing more often and it was slowing the speed people could work at; it was impossible to add customers' orders quickly. Orders were not being processed and customers and staff were unhappy.

Desired result: Resolve the system problems enabling the teams to work effectively and orders to be processed. What steps might be needed to turn this situation around?

Manufacturing example: The cost of specialist technical labour increased, pushing up the cost of manufacture. The customers would resist a price increase and another option had to be found.

Desired result: Source a more cost-effective way of delivering work whilst maintaining quality standards. Retain customers. What steps might be needed to turn this situation around?

Management example: On taking over a new team there were some obvious major challenges: they were demotivated, productivity was down and staff seemed to be leaving more frequently. This was a concern for the customers and the employees.

Desired result: Motivate the team, to encourage productivity. Change the environment to retain team members. What steps might be needed to turn this situation around?

Sales example: Sales were down and customers were tightening their belts; new products weren't proving popular. Everyone was asking for discounts.

Desired result: Increase the number of sales, drive purchase of new products and demonstrate value to the customer. What steps might be needed to turn this situation around?

Task: Why were you selected to change this situation?
What experience did you have that made you the right person?
Had you delivered this type of change before?
Which of your skills and strengths made this easy for you?

Action stations

Remember, you're telling a story; the audience doesn't know the natural thought processes you have gone through when rising to the task. Did the princess ever realise she was more likely to be a victim of kidnapping or poisoning simply from being born into the wrong family? The audience were rooting for someone to come and save her but the journey the hero went on was where the drama occurred.

We took it for granted that the hero would know the route to the castle, embrace the dragon fighting techniques as a natural, and overcome all the other unknown obstacles. The instinctive thought processes that you go through when presented with a challenge are unknown to your audience. If you've worked in an industry for several years, all the knowledge and experience you have gained has become second nature. Everyone in the organisation might know you are the go-to person, always reliable, but now we're talking about 'selling your tell' to a new audience.

What makes you different and special?

I was recently working with Paul, a Facilities Manager, who was working on a contract for a National Health Service Trust. He was very clear that his role was 'to make things work'; by this, he meant ensuring that all the hospital porters and cleaners were where they needed to be. We worked together to understand what "fix it" meant to the organisation. It meant meeting legislation levels on cleanliness and passing the imminent inspection.

When Paul began the contract he utilised his existing knowledge to make a quick impact and drove improvements. He was hit by the mental barrier of 'I was simply doing my job'. I asked Paul what would have happened if it was somebody less experienced who had taken the role. He stated, 'it might have taken longer for them to get results; they may not have been aware of how things work or as used to the processes'. He soon began to realise that his extensive experience was one of the things that made him different and special. You can't put a price on experience.

Once we triggered the right train of thought he began to realise how valuable his experience and knowledge were. One of the first things he did when he arrived was review how things were currently working; he identified where he could make the most impact in the shortest time. Then he identified that the cleaning crew were spending time transporting cleaning materials backwards and forwards to the wards each day. Paul identified that by placing the materials on the wards, in safe and secure environments, he could save an hour per member of staff each day. What did this mean to the organisation? In real terms, it resulted in a saving for the organisation in excess of £600k per annum. Once we took it a stage further and quantified the result he began to realise how one small change had a major impact.

When Paul worked through the different scenarios and began to 'sell his tell' he realised that his 'different and special' was becoming easier to talk about. He understood how to deliver stories so that other people could understand why having him around would mean they had their very own hero. He was providing them with all the evidence they needed to make the right decision and engage him.

Now it's time to sell your tell!

Think about the stories you're most proud of, think about your biggest achievements. This is the perfect place to start; you can dig a little deeper as you begin to create volumes of your success stories.

Exercise Three – Selling your tell

It's time to start formulating your stories, demonstrating your superhero powers and showing how you've made a difference. Considering the skills and strengths you highlighted in the previous exercise; which have you utilised in each of your stories?

Working through each of your achievements in turn think about the challenge you faced and how you solved it – can this be quantified? Think about people, processes and how you have impacted on both. Have you saved time and money, increased efficiency, generated profit, made improvements, retained staff, grown the organisation, downsized, gained market recognition, embedded stability?

This is your chance to shine!

Story One
S Situation

T Task

A Action

R Result

Story Two (and so on....)
S Situation

T Task

A Action

R Result

Summary of Step Three
Be clear about the message you want to market to your potential employers. Remember this is your chance to create a bank of stories to make the process easier. This is the most important homework you will do.

Step Four: Application sensation

Now you have your stories, it's time to put pen to paper. From the previous chapters you'll now be feeling significantly more career conscious, and have the start of a story bank focussing on your key achievements selling your tell. The next step is to transform those stories into a CV or application form that's going to bag you that all-important interview. You do not need to be a wordsmith; however, you do need to sell your tell so the audience can easily see how you will fit the particular role. We are using evidence of past successes to prove future capabilities. Do remember that your reader may not be the person you expect; it could be a recruiter; a HR professional; the direct employer, or a computer. Did the last one surprise you? Your CV or application form has to be so clear that even a non-human will put you on the 'yes' pile. You're limited to words and space - a good CV should only be two pages of A4, so you have to make every single one count.

I see hundreds of CVs every year, and have seen many thousands throughout my career, all of them different but many of them making very similar errors. Even over the last few weeks I've had several people say 'I'm just an Operations Director, accountant, teacher, and so on', and my personal favourite, 'lucky to be in the right place at the right time'. They're hiding behind a job title and need to take it several steps further. Rest assured, you may be an Operations Director, Project Manager, Customer Service Representative, but you will not do exactly what someone else with that job title does. Every one of your stories will be in some way unique, and it's that difference that will either get you an interview or not.

Selling your difference

When you enter the job market there's potentially a lot of competition. There could be hundreds of applicants also fighting for the position you want. When you're reading through hundreds of CVs, it's easier to look for what's not there; at best, your CV or application form may make it on to the maybe pile. Are you taking the time to demonstrate how you're different? What is the 'extra' they get from you?

With this in mind, it's easy to understand that the reader will usually look for reasons not to give you the job, rather than think of reasons why they should give you the job. It's far easier to find a reason to say 'no' than 'yes'. You may not have one of the essential criteria, you may be missing a qualification or specific industry expertise..... the list goes on. You need to ensure that the information makes it easy for them to see why you are right for the role; never expect them to read between the lines.

A CV is a sales tool. It's designed to present your strengths to a potential employer and demonstrate the benefits an organisation will receive by having you on board. Are people as quick to judge your CV as they are to judge you in person? The reality is yes – you do only have a few seconds to make a first impression, either in writing or face to face. So does making your CV stand out mean you're more likely to secure an interview?

Standing out from the crowd – good or bad idea?

I led a discussion about CVs recently, and the perceptions held by potential employers when they receive them. One of the major pet hates that was revealed was the use of 'comic sans' as the chosen font. The majority of people said an overwhelming 'no' when faced with this font; it's perfectly acceptable if you're five years old and writing a poem, not so good if you're CEO of a major organisation. Then came the backlash, regarding 'never judging a book by its cover'....are people right to make an assumption straightaway, based on something as simple as a font? The honest answer is, if your CV stands out to a potential employer for the wrong reasons they're unlikely to read past the personal profile. Times New Roman also received negativity, being deemed old fashioned and dull. WordArt was also frowned upon, as were the people who utilised several different fonts and effects throughout. Arial or Calibri are both acceptable fonts; ensure that the font size is around 11 so that your audience can read it clearly. This does mean that you limit space, but this is fine. Your clearest messages need to be delivered with maximum impact.

Over the years people have tried to make their CV stand out in even bigger ways; when recruiting for salespeople I received a CV printed on a piece of

Perspex; it was a beautiful piece of work and made me take notice; however, there was a flip side. It stood out to me, but what also stood out was that the candidate's heart lay elsewhere; she wanted to be a graphic designer but was looking for an alternative role until she landed her dream career. If I'd been looking for someone in graphic design or another creative discipline she would have had an instant interview, as it was it made the 'no' pile (with the relevant feedback, of course). Other stories I've heard include people using garish paper to ensure their CV was different from the rest of the pile. Although I think one of my favourites was a pastry chef who sent samples with his CV. Think about what is appropriate for your industry. Do consider that most people only expect two sheets of white paper....

Curriculum, Ciraculam, Cer......

The use and appearance of a CV should be in the format most people are familiar with. Understand what job it's supposed to do. It's simply there to get you in front of your next potential employer. Many candidates still feel the need to add a bold CV title to the document, many making the basic mistake of misspelling Curriculum Vitae. This is another blatant way of scuppering the all-important first impressions a potential employer forms. Keep career conscious and remember that you need every bit of space to make your message stand out; the first thing to stand out should be your name. It's about you, so ensure that it's nice and bold at the top: first name and surname is fine, they don't need to know all your middle names at this stage, if ever.

During the discussion I led, the subject of photographs arose. This is very common in parts of Europe and Asia, although the general rule is 'no' when it comes adding a picture of you in the UK job market. Although you may not add a picture to your CV there may be many of you in the public/digital arena for the employer to view; ensure pictures of you online are ones you would feel comfortable they saw. Does your picture on professional social media platforms represent the image you would like to convey? Is it of you and you alone; it may not be the best place for you to display the image of you with your fur baby, or real baby, or worse, simply seeing you as a tiny dot in the background. People will be looking at your online presence.

Gramma and speling....(sorry)

This step should be obvious, right? No one would be so remiss as to forget to check simple things like grammar and spelling throughout their CV, would they? The answer is 'yes', and with some hilarious results. One that springs to mind is a candidate who was talking about driving change; one of the key things he did was restrain the team - he did, of course, mean 'retrain', the other suggests an entirely different management style! The easiest things in the world are to miss a word, use an incorrect word or not spot a spelling error. Not all of us are natural spellers either; that's okay, the answer is to get someone else to proof-read it. I discussed this subject with a recruitment consultant recently who stated, 'I don't change incorrect spellings on a CV before I send it out. I wouldn't want to hoodwink my client'. A recruiter is not there to write your CV for you, they're there to find the best match for the roles they recruit for. Certainly food for thought. One of the biggest assumptions from candidates is that the recruiter is working on their behalf - you couldn't be more wrong. More on the recruitment conundrum later.

Content, content, content

One of my career coaching clients, Geoff, came to me recently, with a CV that was underselling him by a mile. The comprehensive, fifteen-page document started talking about his early success as head boy (he was a senior level executive well into his fifties), then he listed each position he'd held since, with a list of responsibilities rather than achievements. There was certainly no room for him to 'sell his difference' and ensure that he was standing out for the correct reasons. A CV of that length was not going to appeal to the audience; too much information is off-putting - they can always ask for more, if required. If you present them with all the information it gives them less need to interview you. An absolute maximum of three pages should be more than adequate to captivate them and secure that all-important interview.

Selling the tell on paper

As a nation, we're not renowned for our ability to sell ourselves. We tend to hope that people glean more from our words than we make obvious. How likely is it that the reader has time to read between the lines? Most CVs are lucky if they're read past the initial summary. This makes it even more important that every single word is used to sell your tell. In a candidate-led market, where there are more positions than people, this is not as critical; we have not been in that situation for a long time. Now there are potentially hundreds of applicants in competition with you for every position.

Geoff and I went through each of his stories, picking out the key points we wanted to highlight to anyone reading the CV. Step by step we built a powerful document that clearly highlighted those skills and strengths he wanted an employer to utilise, as well as the supporting evidence to show the 'how' and 'why' it mattered. When we worked together to rewrite it he was amazed by the difference. It pitched him at the right senior level, and he said, 'I don't recognise myself'. The document was much clearer, significantly more concise, and written with the reader in mind.

Honestly, you can trust me

Now, there is something I would like to make entirely clear: Geoff's CV was a 100% honest reflection of his career. There was not a hint of over-exaggeration on the document, there weren't any fabrications - we simply highlighted his achievements and presented them in a much clearer way. One of my other clients described CV-writing as a dark art, suggesting, therefore, that there was something mystical about the transformation. Although some people may disagree, there was no magic, simply years of experience.

The reason I mention experience is that many people seem to beat themselves up for not being able to create their own CV. A high number of people I've worked with have never had to create a CV before; they may have worked in the same place for years, sometimes, their entire career. Their exposure to CVs has been from a recruiter's point of view, as they employed people to the lower ranks. Very few people see the CVs of those in senior management. How are you supposed to know how to create a senior level CV when you may never have even seen one?

I genuinely believe that the reason it's simple for someone like me to write a CV that makes an impact is objectivity and impartiality. If you can see each individual as a product to be marketed to a potential buyer, and focus on the key areas to highlight, the rest is straightforward. It's significantly easier than being personally involved. Remove emotional attachment to your stories - the niggling boss, the client who said 'no' to an impressive proposal, the company that is no longer in existence despite your hard work. None of this matters to the reader.

The 'sell' is about the impact you made when you were in that position, not what happened before or after. Geoff provided the perfect example of this: as a consultant he often analysed data, and presented a company with a range of options to improve their performance. This was what he was paid to do. One of the changes he identified had the potential to save the organisation $1million per year. The family-run company decided that the changes were too big and did not implement them - this did not mean he did not deliver on the proposal. The implementation was up to them and out of his control. In the same way than if you secured a major account that was then lost once you left the organisation; highlight the positive and stop at the point control was taken from you.

The headline act - from the top

So what makes a good CV? From the top: start with your name in bold - as I said before, this document is all about you! Personal details: forget about the full address, if someone is going to write to you they can pick up the phone and talk to you first. It's useful to include a town or postcode, though, in case your CV is entered onto a database and they do a radius search. Ensure the contact details you want to be used are on there too: mobile, email, link to professional profiles. Be cautious about such as identity theft, i.e. giving too much information away. At this point, your past salaries are unimportant too, they're just another reason to rule you in or out.

The next section that will capture the interest of the reader is the personal profile - this should be a clear representation of what you've achieved in your roles. What were your key deliverables? Remember that word 'WANT' – what are you wanting to highlight to the reader? Avoid the clichés; if you're a managing director, telling us that you can communicate concisely at all levels is somewhat pointless - we assume you can speak to people to have already had a successful career. You only have a couple of pages and these words are going to influence whether the reader is hooked or not.

How not to do it

'I am a passionate person who gets on well with people and communicates at all levels'.

How to do it

A senior manager with a proven track record of leading teams to achieve goals and objectives.

Notice that there isn't an 'I' – you're a product and presenting an entirely objective view of your skills and achievements. This personal profile is your chance to capture interest, and do remember that you only get a few seconds to make the right first impression. A CV is always written in the past tense too, be careful not to switch between tenses. What are the key elements you want to communicate? If they did not read the rest of your CV what message would that profile hold? Is it selling you as 'special'

and 'different'?

Computer says 'no'!

Have you ever asked yourself how Google seems to know what you're thinking? Can you remember a world before search engines? Keywords became king; CV scanners have been in existence for many years looking for a particular word or skill and pulling it out. This could be a technical skill or a softer skill. The crucial thing to focus on is that it may not be a human reading it. Ensuring you have the right words in your document is imperative. It's acceptable to have a 'key skills' section where you have between 8-10 keywords to make you rank higher in searches. Incredibly clever candidates often change these words to match ones in the advertisement. If you have highlighted what the employer is looking for in your CV then the match would be closer. Although job boards have different algorithms they all rank based on closest matches to specified search criteria. This is all something to keep in mind when creating your powerful marketing tool.

It's all about style

There are two main types of CV: chronological and functional. A reverse chronological style is the preferred one by most recruiters and employers; this means starting with your most recent role and working backwards. I often get asked how far people need to go back; I would always recommend 10-15 years. Anything prior to this you can choose

to exclude. As many assumptions are based on the information contained in your CV, less is definitely more. We all would hope that these assumptions would not limit your chances of securing an interview but we have to be realistic. Limiting how many roles you display means age does not become a factor - a recruiter can rule people in or out based on them being too old or too young. Qualifications are important, however avoid adding the dates!

In terms of the chronological CV, achievements are the most important thing. Back to your stories! Abridged versions of these stories should be enough to solicit interest from a reader. Four or five achievement statements are usually enough to demonstrate the impact you had in each role. We want to raise enough interest and questions for them to need to meet you face to face.

Dysfunctional functional CV

The use of functional CVs is generally deemed less popular to the reader, as it's harder to find the information they need. They do have their place, though. If you're looking to change sector or you need to draw on achievements from earlier in your career, they can be a highly effective way of presenting your stories. The stories need to be grouped into skill areas for example: Business Improvement; Business Development; Project Management, and so on. As I mentioned before, there are uses for this style of CV, such as if you need to demonstrate how transferable your skills are, this can be a clear way to illustrate that.

This is often used by consultants who want to demonstrate case studies. The only other thing you need to add is companies, dates and job titles. In most cases, a reverse chronological style is usually the preferred format.

Learning Japanese, I really think so

So you have sculpted the almost perfect CV, you have created intrigue and interest in your sell and are now simply looking for a face to face meeting to deliver your tell. What about the 'you' outside of work, the social you? Is your CV all about work? Is anyone interested in the part of you that likes mountain biking, fell walking, attending Star Wars' conventions, etc.? Do your interests have a place?

I canvassed a number of Yorkshire-based business leaders and job seekers. The direct employers seem to lean towards adding hobbies and interests to the CV, as it helped them evaluate if the person might fit into their team. If the interests section was omitted, it was still a key question asked at interview stage.

The clear message that came through was that even your interests are challenged by the interviewer. If you say you like reading, ensure you can talk about the last book you read, the same goes with theatre, live music and foreign languages. I always remember at the beginning of my career, back in my recruitment days, having a client who said he was learning Japanese on his CV - it sounded an interesting hobby, and the interviewer thought so too. When he was asked a simple question in Japanese he froze; it turned out it was something he thought would be interesting rather than the truth. As I mentioned early on, everything on your CV should be factual. Don't add interests just for the sake of it, they must be true. Also, consider what your hobbies say about you. It may be that a hobby of yours is a genuine shared interest with the interviewer, helping you to connect on an entirely different level.

Are your interests appropriate? If you have any interests that may be politically difficult then it would be better to exclude them. However, if you do not have much real life work experience, interests can be the difference between securing an interview or not. This is not harking back to the days of the 'old boys' club' and wondering which county you played for, it's about demonstrating a different dimension to you in your CV. Are you, for example, a Non-Exec Director for a charity looking for a transition to the third sector? This type of interest has to be included as it can support the goal you're trying to achieve. However, a single line is enough, do remember that space is of a premium, to give the potential employer just enough so that they want to meet you.

Application sensation – the right form

CVs are not always the preferred style; application forms are utilised, especially by the public sector. They usually list competencies and ask for specific examples that demonstrate a particular skill relevant to the position. Sometimes, an applicant is required to demonstrate an organisational value and how they incorporate this into their competency. I recently worked with Jonathan, who was seeking promotion to Inspector within a UK police force. He had some great examples of his achievements but struggled to shape them into a story that would satisfy the competency and the values. His biggest challenge was assuming that the reader understood his role and would think along the same lines as him; his biggest error of judgement was that they'd read between the lines.

With application forms you're often restricted to a specific word count, and you may not be clear in how the competency criteria is measured. Therefore, it's crucial to ensure every single word makes the correct impact. When we reworked Jonathan's competencies by answering the questions, they became much stronger. Tying in the organisational values became easy. The result of this reworking ensured he scored the highest mark possible for each competency and secured his promotion.

The application form and CV are simply one step towards getting you through the door and ensure you get the chance to speak to the decision maker. The only supporting information you can provide are personal statements or cover letters. These are further opportunities to demonstrate how you're a good fit to the role, organisation and culture. Never send an untailored cover letter; be clear and concise and highlight your salient achievements.

If you're creating a personal statement, go back to selling your tell. At this point, you may be concerned that you do not have enough stories; you should continue to develop your STAR examples as you progress through your career, I would say one or two per month. They are a brilliant tool for appraisals, and ensure you remain career conscious. Always have an up to date CV.

The Cover Story

Sometimes you are required to provide a little extra in the form of supporting information; including personal statements or cover letters. It is important that you see these as a further opportunity to demonstrate how you're a good fit to the role, organisation, and culture. Never make the mistake of sending an untailored cover letter; be clear and concise and highlight your salient achievements. Pick out the requirements from the advert or specification and highlight how you match these; the clearer you make the link between you and the role; the easier it is for the reader to see you as a match.

Some organisations may ask for a supporting personal statement, remember to go back to selling your tell and using more of your success stories. At this point, you may be concerned that you do not have enough stories; you should continue to regularly develop your STAR examples as you progress throughout your career. My recommendation would be to develop say one or two examples per month. They are also a brilliant tool to be utilised in one to ones or appraisals, they are crucial in ensuring you remain 100% career conscious. Remember to always have an up to date CV.

BATMAN

Gotham Tel: 911 bat Email: bat@batman

A dedicated superhero with a proven track record in driving down high crime levels across a sprawling metropolis; influencing cultural change, including engaging with police officials, the mayor, and other stakeholders, increasing health and safety whilst providing exceptional stunt skills. High technical competence generating ideas and creating innovative solutions. Led a small domestic support team.

Crime Fighting * Communication * Technology
Employee Motivation * Problem Solving * Influencing * Secret Keeping

Gotham City; New Jersey   **2000- 2014**
A sprawling metropolis with over a million inhabitants

Superhero/Antihero
Engaged by Gotham to implement a crime reduction strategy utilising a variety of complex tactics to ensure safety of inhabitants.

- Devised and embedded plan to defeat the control of Gotham by evil villains such as Penguin, The Joker and Poison Ivy. Resulted in maintaining a 0% takeover rate of the city that kept all inhabitants safe

Exercise Four: Application Sensation

It's time to become your own superhero! Your CV is your marketing document, and your first chance to make an impression. It's your way of generating interest and getting employers to pick up the phone and speak to you. There's no point trying to revamp an old document; throw it away, this superhero deserves a brand new comic (I'll stop...)

1. Ka Pow – get them interested. Create a 5 - 6 profile summary highlighting your proven achievements; keep conscious about the areas you would want to talk about in an interview situation.
2. Zlonk (come on, when else am I going to get to use that word?!) - Select the keywords you think will get you the best results from people and machines.
3. Organise your dates in reverse chronological order – start selling your stories!

Summary of Step Four

Remember: A CV should be no more than two A4 pages – use the past tense and limit the amount of information you give away. It's only about generating interest.

Check it! Then check it again and ask someone else to check it. Be honest - everything in there can be verified. Keep a focus on the positive. Always have an up to date CV.

Step Five: Let's talk the talk

Now you have the perfect CV, the next logical step is being called to interview. Evidence, evidence, evidence seems to have been the moral of your story so far. How can you prove that you're the right person for the job? It's all well and good having a sensational set of stories in the toolbox, but what happens when it comes to talking about them? Nothing strikes fear into our hearts like the word 'interview'. It can be a pressure cooker; people are aware they only have a short time to impress, which only adds to the stress.

The key thing to remember about interviews is that the best candidate does not always secure the position – it's the candidates that *portray* themselves as the best that do. Think about colleagues you've worked with over the years: are there any you believe MUST have been good at interviews, as they appear less than competent in their actual role? I asked a number of professionals about their worst interview experiences as candidate and employer - some were hilarious, some disturbing, but they were all true!

Candidate conundrum

A client mentioned to me that when they were interviewing for an office junior, a very nice young lady arrived with her mum in tow. The mum then proceeded to answer every single question on her daughter's behalf. At the crucial moment Mum then commented, 'my daughter is a real chatterbox, who never shuts up!', though she hadn't uttered a word throughout the interview. I mentioned this story whilst in a network meeting with a recruiter, who confirmed candidates turn up with parents with startling regularity. I think I can forgive the candidate but what are the parents thinking? What I found even funnier was that turning up with additions is certainly not limited to parents; candidates have also arrived with their significant others, children and the odd cuddly toy thrown in for good luck!

'Not a personal experience, but once worked at a software company where a candidate turned up with a teddy bear (wearing its own suit!). Bizarrely, she got the job, and the teddy bear proceeded to go everywhere with her throughout her career, with different outfits for different occasions......' **Peter B**

It suits the wearer, nae the starer

The above line was something my dear grandma used to say, alluding to the fact that you dress for yourself and not the people looking at you. A beautiful sentiment, Grandma, but perhaps one best left out of the interview scenario. All too often, people do not consider that the interviewer will make a judgement based on that first impression. As a recruiter, one of the first candidates I sent for interview arrived in full biker leathers, I never ever made the same mistake of not telling them to go suited and booted again. I've heard several stories about skirts being too short, trousers ripping, too much makeup and erroneous aromas, both pleasant and some not-so pleasant. Remember to dress in a professional manner so that you look and feel confident, and you're sure you're portraying the right impression.

'I went for an interview at Woolworths to work on the supply side. Just as the interview was about to start, the manager/interviewer said that they'd just had a delivery, and would I help, as they needed to get the stock into the store. I had a quick think and thought 'okay'. Got downstairs to find that it was a load of cheeses, smelly ones to boot! Needless to say my suit did not come through the experience well, but I did get the job!' **Steve B**

The story I still use to this day, as a benchmark for how bad an interview can go, belongs to an old career coaching client, Una. She opted to drive rather than catch a train, then bumped her car in the car park. Obviously, she got incredibly upset and went into the toilets to calm herself down. There, the door handle came off in her hand - she had to call her husband and ask him to call the company (she hadn't brought the contact details). She was finally released and introduced to the interviewer, who - you've guessed it - was the owner of the vehicle she bumped! If you can top that, please do get in touch!

The challenges do not just fall in the laps of the interviewees, the interviewers need to consider their style too and make questions clear enough for the candidate to understand. One interviewer asked a school–leaver, 'what gets you up on a morning?' To which he gave the literal response: 'my mum, with a cup of tea'. This, to all intent and purpose, was the right answer. Honesty has a lot to answer for in the interview process. That said, I once offered a young girl called Claire a job based on the fact that she admitted she was late for an interview as she had got caught up in a chapter of Harry Potter. I am proud to say she was one of the best hires I ever made.

Asking ambiguous questions results in a laborious interview for both parties. A good interview should be a two-way process where the candidate decides if the job is right for them as much as the employer deciding if the candidate is right for the role. All too often, as the job search drags on, it becomes more about the need to secure any job, and candidates can often appear desperate. In this two-way process, though, the interviewer can also get it completely wrong.

A company can let itself down by coming across as being unprofessional or disorganised. Very few people in the UK have been trained to interview effectively. People have been asked inappropriate questions at interview, on religion, sexuality or their likelihood of having children. The interview can also prove an exercise for the interviewer to flex their ego!

Here are a couple of examples where the interviewer gets it completely wrong.

'Making a candidate comfortable is difficult to some, like the guy that interviewed me at 10:17am.

Not before, not after. He sat in a seat on a raised platform so the sun shined (at exactly 10:17 AM) through a window behind him right onto your face. A picture of the queen looked on from another wall, which served to increase the pressure. He looked crestfallen when he was unable to move the seat he'd sat me in – I couldn't be certain, but I'm sure it was glued to the floor – I stood up and paraded round answering his questions. Thus, no job offer – thank goodness!' **Phil W**

'I applied for a really good job with a really good company, and was looking forward to the interview and finding out more about the role. After waiting for 15 minutes, the receptionist said they could not get hold of the person to interview me and if I could come back in an hour. After an extra hour of mental preparation, I met my interviewer and had the normal questions, and our chat went well. I was asked to do an assessment, followed by the final interview. On completing the assessment, the interviewer did a disappearing act again and left for the day. The receptionist was very pleasant and indicated that I could arrange another meeting for the final interview. I wish the interviewer was honest with me that he had other priorities and I would have rescheduled. Therefore, instead of learning more about the company and role, it actually succeeded in putting me off the company altogether.' **Stephen B**

A common theme from stories I've been told seems to be the poor behaviour of the interviewer: running late, forgetting candidates are attending, leaving the room without explanation - and the biggest bug bear: an interviewer being obviously uninterested in what the candidate had to say. Andy actually had an interviewer fall asleep during his interview. How should candidates react in these situations? I genuinely believe if a company cannot treat you properly at the interview stage, there's a good chance that the organisation is not the one for you. See it as a lucky escape.

First, second, third...

Remember, most people will go for a number of interviews before they secure the right position, and the more senior the position the more stages you should expect within the process. It's not uncommon to have three or four different stages from telephone interviews: meet the team, technical tests, and psychometrics, and in some cases, a full assessment day. These stages are crucial for you too; you'll be able to assess whether the company can offer you everything you need. You visualised your perfect role, do they hit the mark on all your criteria? The more stages you go through, the more you can build a fuller picture of what it would really be like to work for them. You're portraying the best version of you, and the company are likely to be doing the same.

Psychometric testing is often like delving into the unknown. If you have never completed one you may worry that you don't know if the answers are right or wrong. The approach should be that there is no right or wrong; it depends on the job role, and the team fit that they're looking for. This is not the experience everyone has, however.

'I had a salesman visit me a couple of years ago to do a presentation on Psychometric Evaluation tests for candidates. He suggested I take the test so that I could see how well the evaluation matched my own assessment of myself. The test was about 30 minutes on a PC, after which, he was disappointed to have to tell me that the results were 'inconclusive'. He assured me, 'no problem. That happens sometimes, a second test invariably produces a result'. So I did another test. Guess what? It was inconclusive again. Perhaps the fact that I was being completely honest, and considering candidates probably wouldn't be as open, confused the software. The upshot is, I don't use psychometric evaluation when interviewing.'
Stuart T

The best thing to do is relax and answer the questions as honestly as you can; this way, you're likely to get accurate results. It's quite rare nowadays for a company to only use the results of a psychometric test or profile to rule you in or out. The tests are not limited to psychometrics, candidates are often asked to complete verbal or numerical reasoning, and in some cases, companies will use graphology to analyse your handwriting. There are many online examples concerning the different types of tests. A company should give you prior notice of anything you'll face in the interview scenario.

Prepare, prepare, and prepare some more

I am always surprised that some candidates do little or no preparation before they attend an interview. When did you last complete detailed preparation for interviews? By preparation, I mean much more than a cursory look at a company website, or printing off a P & L, or peeking at their social media trail. How can you be sure that you're talking the talk, what message do you want them to understand about you? Interviews are not rocket science; there certainly shouldn't be any surprises. Lists of questions are freely available, and if you consider that there are very few questions they can ask you, preparation should be straightforward.

Questions and answers

There is a limited number of questions you can be asked in an interview scenario. Common ones are: tell me about a time something went to plan, a time something went wrong, a difficult person or situation you had to handle, your strengths and weaknesses.... Every time I complete interview role play with my clients they say, 'I should have known that question was going to be asked'. If they'd put time aside to think about it they would have been more prepared. You can probably make a list of the common questions you've been asked at previous interviews. The skill now is to take the evidence from the 'selling your tell' and match a story that will prove you're the right person for the job.

The first question you're likely to be asked is to

summarise your career - to talk through your CV, or to tell them a little about yourself. Now you're career conscious, you should have a clear idea of the key points you would like to put across in this statement. What are your career highlights? What would you like the interviewer to focus on? Keep in mind that this is a two-way street, you only need to answer the questions you want to answer. The more you shape the interview, the more chance you get to present your evidence. Are you ready to start your practice?

First things first; ensure you have the perfect interview outfit, your shoes are clean, and everything you carry with you portrays the right kind of image. Buy a new shirt or top - it may help you feel more confident; carry a nice pen, wear a nice watch, and please leave your parents and soft toys at home.

Exercise Five: Let's Talk the Talk

Work your way through the following questions, matching one of the stories from your toolkit to ensure that you're providing evidence of your achievement.

Q) Tell me about yourself

Keep it relevant, keep it recent, signpost the themes you want to discuss in the interview. What experiences and expertise do you want the interviewer to focus on? Formulate a two to three minute statement (sometimes referred to as an elevator pitch). The trick is to practice, practice, practice. Imagine how confident you will feel when you can deliver a slick and considered response to the first question. This will certainly set the tone for the interview. This is the perception you want to portray. The more you can demonstrate the competencies they're looking for you to display in the role, the easier it is for them to choose you.

Q) Why did you leave your last role?

The Seven Steps to Career Consciousness are all about focussing on the positives within your career and striving towards the role you desire. The word 'positive' is key here, however you present information to a potential employer it must remain positive. No interviewer wants to hear how badly treated you were in a previous role or how disorganised the company were, how your manager treated you unfairly, or any other negatives. In the earlier chapters we highlighted that change can be forced upon you; therefore, thinking how you're going to present this in a positive light may be even trickier.

Q) Are you happy with your career to date?

What are they asking for here - more negatives? Expect these types of questions and practice smiling and giving positive answers. They're looking for sensitive areas to explore. Keep your guard up!

Q) What are your strengths/weaknesses/has your work ever been criticised?

So really what they are saying is 'give me a reason to employ or not employ you'. Remain conscious of the positives; you're not going to tell them any of the clichés like: 'I'm a perfectionist', 'I work too hard' - no one believes you. Never be frightened to turn the question around on them, i.e. how would they help you overcome a shortfall in knowledge on products or systems? Remember, it's a game - they may not be the world's best interviewer!

Q) Tell us a time something went well/went badly

The interviewer is giving you the perfect opportunity to impart one of your hero stories, or a time you fixed a scenario that went badly. Dig into your toolkit, you can never present them with too much evidence. Never ever tell them of a time something went wrong and you didn't find a solution!

Q) Where do you see yourself in one, three, five years' time?

Without a crystal ball it's impossible to answer this type of question, so turn it around and ask them how they see the role developing. Most importantly, it's essential that you recognise an interview is simply a business conversation. You're looking to find synergy between both parties.

Q) If you were a superhero, what power would you choose?

No, I am not obsessed with superheroes - this was a genuine question directed to one of my clients. Quirky questions do not have a place in an interview. I'd suggest, in such a situation, that you again turned the question back on to the interviewer, with a response such as this: 'It would be interesting to know what powers already exist within the organisation so I could identify where there might be a gap'. The same goes for what animal/fruit/season you might be, and all other strange questions.

The more familiar you are with the types of questions you can be asked, the easier it is to prepare responses. You'll begin to notice that a lot of the questions are very similar, they're just phrased differently.

Competent competency-based interviewing

Now that you're getting the hang of selling your tell through the stories in your toolkit, answering competency-based questions should be fairly straightforward. In a competency-based interview they will ask you for specific examples.

Q) Decision making: Can you tell me about a situation where you had to solve a problem or make a decision that required careful thought. What did you do?

Here, they're asking for the specific details – you're already prepared as it's not dissimilar to the 'tell me a time something went wrong' question.

Q) Influence: Describe a recent situation in which you convinced an individual or a group to do something, and the steps you took.

As you can see, one of your STAR stories can be used here too. Spend some time cross-referencing your stories with the type of questions you're likely to be asked. One of my clients recorded a list of questions onto an MP3 and plays them in the car. Nothing is likely to take him by surprise. The more comfortable you are with your stories, the more relaxed you will feel. If you are relaxed you will exude confidence.

An interviewer may try and push your buttons, with statements such as 'I feel like you may be a little overqualified'. These tricky statements can be left hanging in the air. As your confidence increases you may simply smile before responding in a considered manner. The interview process is just a game, learn to play it.

Summary of Step Five
Remember: Interviews are simply business conversations. The more you're prepared to answer difficult and sensitive questions, the more confident you will feel.

Step Six: Recruiters, rejection and networking

Steps one to five should see you ready for anything, your tool kit bursting with achievements, your documents dazzling and your interview technique sharper than a cut throat razor......now what? Now is the time to go out there and create opportunities to form a plan, to ensure you remain in control of the whole process.

RIP traditional job search

May you rest in peace, traditional job market. It's true that the market has shifted a long way from the days when the newspaper was king for the job seeker. Do you remember those halcyon days of knowing which day of the week was best to scour the adverts for your next opportunity? It makes me remember the Yorkshire Evening Post's street vendors who would call out when it was job day on a Thursday. Over the years the pages have become thinner and thinner; if it has been a number of years since you last searched for a job today may seem like a whole new world. The internet seems to have taken over, new job boards are still popping up daily - so how do you know which one to choose? Check and measure its performance to ensure you maximise the return on your time.

Internet ranting

The internet makes it very easy for you to become a busy fool, spending time feeling like you're being productive, which brings us on to job boards and aggregates. How do the job boards fare when it comes to being career conscious? Job boards perform differently, depending on which market sector you're in, some of the specialist sites are a great place to start identifying the buoyancy of the market; the internet is still number one when it comes to being a research tool. Who are the recruiters and companies you should be speaking to?

One of the critical mistakes made by job seekers is to spend too long trawling through irrelevant jobs on inappropriate sites. Job boards are not all things to all men; the creators have a specific demographic in mind. Some are for lower level jobs and others, executive level, and various ones in-between. Spending hours searching through lists will not 'create opportunity', it can lull you into thinking you're being active when, in fact, you're wasting precious time. An active job seeker with a clear and conscious strategy will only spend 20-30 minutes a day checking both job boards and aggregates; setting up accurate alerts can save you time in the long run. The rest of your time should be spent being proactive and remaining career conscious. Time spent in front of a PC should be minimal, being out in the market and having good business conversations is a sure-fire way to succeed.

Once your CV is uploaded onto a job board, you should receive a flurry of interaction from the recruiters. Any new CVs that are added are automatically emailed straightaway so they're aware of your 'special and different'. This immediate activity can lure you into a false sense of security, believing that your job search is starting to build momentum. All too often this activity is short-lived and the phone stops ringing, use these conversations as only one strand of your job search, not the be all and end all. Remember to keep a track of who you spoke to and when.

Keep conscious of everything you prepared in steps three and four. Do you have the right keywords in the body of the text? Is your profile strong enough to capture the interest of your audience? Is it giving them enough information to spark their interest, yet not so much information that they do not need to pick up the phone and speak to you? Is your CV selling your achievements, or is it still as if you're reading a job specification? Are you rehearsed and ready to talk the talk? Does your 'tell me about yourself' roll off your tongue.

Live and direct

Companies often advertise their own positions on job boards too. Imagine the moment that a potential employer recognises the need for a new recruit and they start to consider all the attributes they're looking for in an 'ideal candidate'; the list becomes longer and longer. It moves from being a personal profile or job specification to a wish list - suddenly they're looking for the perfectly-shaped square peg for their square hole. This makes it very difficult for the candidate and recruitment companies to be a match. Will they ever find the perfect candidate? In this case, the fairytale does not exist, and there's no such thing as the perfect candidate; however, there is such a thing as the perfectly prepared candidate. As I mentioned previously, it's the candidate who portrays themself as the best who will ultimately secure the job.

Never be put off if you're looking at a job specification and feel that there are some skills you're lacking. The advert may just be a wish list; some of the skills may be critical to the role whilst others may simply be desirable. It's certainly worth applying if there are only a couple of gaps; it's quite likely that the candidates who are your competition have a couple of gaps too. It's always more attractive to a company to recruit directly as they're able to save the recruitment fee. The money is better being added to your salary than lining the pocket of a recruitment consultant.

The recruitment process does not always go 100% smoothly. Sometimes the interview process stalls and the company decides to put a particular job on hold. There is often a raft of excuses as to why the process does not continue. 'We decided to fill it internally.' A colleague may have withdrawn their resignation meaning the company no longer needs to recruit. A company may decide to start the recruitment process, ready to replace a problem individual, then after interviewing a few candidates decide the grass is not always greener. The recruitment process could have been a fact-finding mission, or they may realise their wish list is impossible, or there's simply been a change in their finances.

Even when the recruitment process goes to plan it can take several months from start to finish; losing momentum is very common. Even if you receive a job offer and contract, nothing is set in stone. I heard of a gentleman who accepted a position only to arrive on the start date to have had the offer revoked. The job market has been turbulent through the recession, and situations and outcomes have been difficult to plan. Accepting an offer does not mean that you take your eye off the market. The scenario I outlined above is not common, however, it's best to keep a focus on your needs and never take your eyes off the market.

Shoot the recruiter

Now before we begin, I'm going to make one thing clear: there are some good recruiters out there providing an excellent service to both their clients and candidates. However, they're the exception rather than the rule. In my years of experience I have yet to hear much good said about the profession from job seekers. I mentioned the flurry of calls from recruiters then the silence, this approach seems to have become the norm. One of the biggest frustrations I hear from job seekers is that recruiters never call them back. Candidates feel that they're fed a string of lies, spiel from the recruiter about 'working on their behalf', and many felt the recruiter was simply pumping them for information, especially pertaining to interviews they might be having. Do remember that recruiters are sales people, they're there to make their own commission, not work to find you your ideal role. By being a highly desirable candidate you can improve your chances of building a relationship with a recruiter and increase your chances of being put in front of one of their clients.

The recruiter should be your point of contact throughout the application process; they're supposed to brief you on the role and negotiate on your behalf when an offer comes in. I often ask clients if they're sure they want to relinquish control. I would always encourage people to negotiate their own deals unless you're confident the recruiter has an edge you don't have. Also remember you might not be the only candidate they have going for interview, you could be one of many. Using recruiters is a necessary evil and an avenue that should not be ignored, however, as with the rest of the traditional advertised market, dealing with them tends to be a reactive rather than proactive approach. If you're not convinced by the above, try and remember the last time a recruiter called you when they said they would.

Behind the smoke and mirrors

There seems to be a great deal of smoke and mirrors surrounding the unadvertised job market. Statistics are bandied about suggesting that anywhere between 70-80% is somehow hidden. Hundreds of my clients over the years have said, 'I've never had to job search before, jobs have always found me'. If this is true, then why is it difficult for some people to believe that a proportion of jobs never make it to the public domain? It's commonplace for a hiring manager to look internally first, then ask employees if they know someone who might be able to do the job. This is a common sense approach as it reduces advertising costs and cuts out the recruitment consultants. It makes perfect sense.

At the executive end of the market it's commonplace for a new CEO or Managing Director to surround themself with a team they trust. During mergers and acquisitions entire management teams can be replaced – again, this makes perfect commercial sense. This type of move can often lead to people being displaced or made redundant in favour of a fresh set of eyes. We know these jobs were never advertised, there was no job spec to box tick. We can soon see how the unadvertised market takes shape and how this hidden 80% is suddenly common sense and the obvious way to recruit.

Let's look closer at companies handling 'sensitive' situations; these positions have to be kept under the radar, perhaps the person being displaced is still unaware. On a more positive note, they may not have even realised they needed someone to come into the business and improve things before they spoke to you. The unadvertised market is alive and well, and continues to help people secure their next position or contract. Do remember, in difficult economic times, there's no such thing as a permanent contract, simply a contract without an end date. Be flexible to agree a mutually beneficial outcome; an increasing number of people are developing portfolio careers where they're working as, or on, more than one thing at once.

The unadvertised market is about leveraging your contacts and defining a proposition that the employer needs. Do your family and friends know what you do? It sounds a strange question but we quite often know a person's job title yet are unclear as to what they do and the impact they have in their role. Now you're career conscious, have you taken the time to educate your family, friends and network contacts regarding what, specifically, you're looking for? Do they understand what you have delivered? Step out from behind the job title and get ready to spread your message.

Network, network, network

You're aiming to take control and remain conscious. You are being 100% proactive and shaping every aspect of your career. The key to taking control and accessing the unadvertised market is networking. Now, before you reel in horror and imagine a room full of awkward-looking people brandishing business cards, that's not true networking. The term is often thrown around but what does it actually mean to you? Networking can take place anywhere, it can be a useful conversation on a commuter train, a chance meeting in a pub, bumping into an old colleague you haven't seen in a while, a professional body you've joined but not investigated. I mentioned that interviews are simply business conversations, networking is the same.

One key myth I need to dispel is that networking is NOT picking up your phone and calling your closest friends and ex-colleagues, asking them if they know of a position; this is the equivalent of burning your contacts. All that will happen if you burn your contacts is that they will feel guilty for not being able to help you. Networking is a mutual exchange and not a 'one hit' communication. It takes time to build a network and you must be prepared to develop these relationships, and even more importantly, you must continue to network even when you've secured your next position. Networking must become a way of life until the day you retire.

Take the time to identify people who may be useful in your job search, those who might know someone in the right industry. Perhaps someone who may be able to talk to you about the type of role you're looking for. Ask your network contacts for things they can help you with, i.e. industry knowledge, additional contacts and advice. Networking is not about asking for a position, it's about building mutually beneficial relationships and getting on the radar of decision makers. Keep in mind it would be extraordinary to make contact at the exact time they were looking for someone like you. This doesn't mean that they will not have a position for you in the future; that's why we build long-lasting relationships.

One of my most memorable success stories about networking came from Darren, a client several years ago; he was one of the least convinced regarding networking I'd come across. He was very much of the mindset that those who knew him would always remember him and let him know about opportunities. He bumped into an old friend at a party and mentioned his job search. He'd recently applied for a role as a project manager with a leading high street bank, it had been an advertised vacancy and he thought nothing more of it. During his conversation with his old friend work came up, and it turned out this friend worked at said bank. He suddenly realised that he hadn't kept in contact with many people so perhaps they were not keeping him at the forefront of *their* minds.

After the party his friend popped along to see HR; they told him that they'd had such an unprecedented response that they would not be able to read all the applications - they simply had a 'yes' and a 'no' pile. It was a matter of who was the best fit, but there was also an element of luck! After his friend had a quick chat with HR, his application made the correct pile. He was called for interview and secured the role! A casual comment turned into an influential move by his friend. Darren made a concerted effort to say thank you to his friend. This is an important point: remember to keep feeding back into your network. Help them out where you can and keep feeding the relationship.

Network fail

There is often reluctance to network, as people are often frightened that they cannot offer something of value, or that a recommendation may reflect on them in some way. Most professional business people will not hold a recommendation against someone. Another client, David, was looking to make a transition into a new sector; a friend of his put him in touch with someone who had the potential to open doors for him in the insurance world. He went along for a 'no strings attached' meeting with the insurance contact; the meeting went well and he was offered a position within the company. This made his friend a bit nervous, and David had to assure him that it would never reflect on him. A few months later, the business changed direction and David was made redundant. His network contact may have passed the buck in terms of responsibility but this didn't impact on their friendship. This type of scenario isn't common, though, most networking is a positive experience.

Network success

There are other ways to network effectively without relying on family and friends. Who are the leading people in your industry, whose knowledge would add value to your search? As long as you make it clear you do not expect them to know of a position for you, people are generally prepared to share knowledge and experience. I mentioned time on the internet, researching people who can make an impact on your job search is a must. Be creative in your approach, avoid email - perhaps try a formal letter asking for a short meeting. One of my London-based clients, Sean, retains the record; he identified five influencers he wanted to approach, created beautifully tailored letters explaining why he wanted to pick their brains, and importantly, what was in it for them; he was influential, in terms of his specialist market knowledge. He secured five out of five meetings, arranged further meetings from the names he garnered, and soon found a new position. This was many years ago and he still is effectively networking to this day. Sean has a position lined up before he leaves his current role. He really is the master of being 100% proactive.

Networking works at any level, you don't have to be an executive or director. It could be your first position or your twenty-first, people can introduce you to others who can impact on your job search in a positive way. Whilst you're not hiding behind a PC, and you're having good conversations, you're being proactive rather than reactive. Spread your net wide, who are the important people locally, who is well connected, are there professional organisations that could help, alumni, professional bodies and conferences? Think about the parents at your children's school, or the friends of your parents; the possibilities are endless. All of these are potential network contacts if you choose to engage with them.

You are now completely conscious and in control of your career, and taking steps to ensure that your dream job is within your grasp. A network contact may not be the magic link for your next position, it may be the one after that, or the one after that. Keep in touch with everyone within your network, keep building relationships. As I said before, this has to be a conscious change so that you continue to network from now until the time you choose to retire. One final point on networking: it really does work. On a personal note, I cannot thank my network enough for helping me build a successful business.

Exercise Six: Recruiters; rejection & networking

Time to identify all the people who may be useful to you; remember, you never know who people know. Once you have a starting point you can proactively develop your network.

1. Create a list of all your close friends who you think may know someone useful for you to speak to.
2. Make a list of family members who you think may know someone useful for you to speak to.
3. Practise telling them about your career goals; the more they can verbalise this for themselves, the easier it is for them to introduce you to useful people.
4. Identify 10-15 local people whom you would like to make contact with over the coming weeks.
5. Create a list of people you come into contact with in your social circle.
6. Identify any industry or regional networking opportunities; conferences, seminars, networking

events; workshops. Every conversation can be useful

7. Identify ten organisations you're interested in approaching and tailor a networking approach letter. Remember to ensure they know what's in it for them.

8. Create a useful method for following up on your entire network - a spreadsheet or diary will ensure no potential opportunity is missed.

Summary of Step Six

Remember: networking is being completely in control of your job search and 100% proactive. You never know who somebody knows; these relationships are building blocks for the future.

Step Seven: Be kind to your mind

The final step I consider to be one of the most important when it comes to the job search process. Steps 1-6 have armed you with all the practical tools you need to refocus and take your new clearly defined and polished product to market (i.e. yourself). You've shaped your vision of what you want and created a checklist to ensure you're getting what you need from your next move. Keep career conscious and in control by ensuring your criteria is clearly defined. You should feel more confident now your toolkit is overflowing with powerful and positive achievement stories. Practice these stories to ensure they remain at the forefront of your mind; you need to be ready for every eventuality.

You have in your hands a sensational CV that is going to captivate audiences, coupled with your honed, killer interview techniques. You've formulated a structured plan to ensure you're being 100% proactive in your job search, or have your step by step plan in place. Now, you're ready to go, and are aware of everything you need to do to remain in control until the day you retire. You need to review your options every couple of years; keep your CV up to date, and remain conscious.

The job search is very much a rollercoaster ride of rejection and being told that you are not the perfect fit; more so, if you're reacting to the advertised market. There are a million and one excuses...I mean reasons...why you might not be the right person for the role. Too old, too young, inexperienced, not experienced enough, someone else had more relevant industry experience, and that's just the start. None of these have to be the honest answer, they're simply an easy way for the recruiter to break bad news. As legislation gets tougher on things like equality, saying 'no' becomes harder for the employer, unless they have a valid reason. Stay positive and do not take the rejection personally; remember, in most cases, it's simply a platitude.

So, why is this chapter called 'be kind to your mind'? As you'll be aware of by now, I firmly believe that your mental state has a major impact on the success or failure of a proactive job search. Being kind to your mind and focusing on the positives will ensure you build up much needed resistance to the trials and tribulations of the search. A good, strong network can take a long time to develop, which can be frustrating. Sometimes it may feel like you are taking one step forward and two steps back. Remember your job search may be the central focus of your mind, but this does not automatically make it a priority for others.

This book has taken you step by step on a journey; you've held up a mirror to yourself and seen what a unique, special and different individual you are. If you're having a down day, go back to step one and re-read the extensive list of skills and strengths you compiled; you have to see the value you offer to the world; that starts with you believing in yourself. It won't be long before someone else recognises the value you can offer to an organisation. You only need one job!

Now that you are 100% focussed and being more strategic in your job search, it means that you limit the amount of rejection you're likely to face. If you find yourself applying for jobs that are not a good fit you're simply increasing the number of times someone will say 'no' to you. Repeated rejection can really wear a person down; this was most definitely the case for one of my past clients, Nick.

Nick had enjoyed a long and successful career in land purchasing, then the recession hit and he was made redundant. Over a two-year period he applied for hundreds of positions. He had a few interviews but the vast majority were rejections, or worse, no response or acknowledgement at all. When we began working together his motivation was less than zero. In the time he'd been out of work he'd resigned himself to the fact he may never have another 'career job'. He began to drive a private hire taxi for income. As is characteristic of Nick, everything he does he does with an air of perfectionism; his taxi was spotless and he always wore a tie. His customers loved him too. This wasn't working for Nick though. He'd been a land buyer for over twenty years and that was his real passion. He could never get the same level of satisfaction driving a private hire vehicle.

Technically, there was nothing wrong with his CV, and he could answer any industry-related question at interview, but the ones that triggered his sensitive spots were harder to deal with. I can remember the session where he said, 'I feel like I've been thrown away'. It was heart-breaking. He went on to explain how his family had rallied round and tried to keep him upbeat. It didn't work; though they loved him no matter what job he did, it was his internal wrangle that affected him. He'd always been the provider, the breadwinner, and now felt useless. He'd all but given up on applying for jobs, and as for networking, his confidence was on the floor, so it was a non-starter. What was the answer?

It's not all about the words

The thing that stood out to me was how Nick carried himself, his head was hung low and a smile only ever flitted across his lips momentarily. For a man over six feet tall he didn't seem to recognise his presence. When it comes to interviews and networking much of your message is communicated through your body language. Who would you rather employ, someone who smiles and makes eye contact and who offers a firm handshake, or the opposite? Remember to talk in a controlled manner, you never want to come across as desperate, so listen more than you talk; answer a question then pause and allow the interviewer to speak. The same goes for networking; if you're in a room full of people, smile, you'll be amazed how many people gravitate towards you, and you'll find it easy to start a conversation. In our sessions we worked as much on how he delivered his message as much as the content of what he said.

Time to refocus

Recognising that his state of mind was holding him back, we slowly began to reprogram his thoughts. We created a toolkit of his stories and began to restore his confidence in his career achievements; starting to talk about the positives again changed his perspective. It had been such a long time since he'd been through the process of 'selling his tell' that he'd forgotten his own value. Over a number of sessions we restored his faith in what he had to offer to the marketplace. I remember the afternoon he called to tell me he had an interview for a land buyer role, he was somewhat nervous to say the least. We agreed to have a session to run through his interview techniques; there's nothing like turning up the heat with role play. His eyes regained their sparkle and his smile was genuine; he had a good feeling about it.

When he went for the interview I waited for news. He'd prepared brilliantly and was genuinely passionate about the project. I'm sure you can guess the outcome. I was never going to end this book on a negative note! Yes, he secured the job, and as I recall, I was on a train to London when I took the call and cheered loudly. He'd worked so hard to be kind to his mind and to change his perspective, within a few weeks he'd secured the success he deserved. Nick stated the first thing he was going to do when he received his first salary payment was to take his wife out for a celebratory dinner to thank her for her support.

Make job searching the day job

Be kind to your mind, set yourself a plan to ensure that you're keeping proactive and are doing a mixture of all necessary job search activities. You do not need to be sat behind a PC to be creating opportunities, some of your best ideas may come to you whilst walking in the woods, playing golf, baking cakes. Build into your plan time to enjoy yourself too. There's little you can do outside working hours and you still need fun and relaxation. Remember that people can often offer you nuggets of advice without having any idea of what you're doing. Smile and don't get defensive, they probably feel pretty useless and are simply trying to help.

Talking to the people around you can be of the greatest help; although remember that they are not an expert in your job search. You are now ready to be your own coach. They may feel that they are giving you the best support they can but the advice can often make people feel defensive. I can remember talking to a Senior Exec and his wife consistently told him he should be going to the job centre. He knew that this was futile from his previous experience. Once he realised his wife was trying to be supportive he stopped taking it personally and simply carried on with his own job search journey. The same goes if you are distracting yourself with a list of urgent jobs that need completing in the home; your job search is your number one focus anything else must be completed around it. Everyone seems to think they're a career expert, yet you already have the vital seven steps towards career consciousness; you just now to need to put them into action.

The working wonder

Even if you're in full or part time work, you need to ensure that you have a clear plan you can stick to. Keep focussed on your goals. You may not have much time to spend on research or networking, so spend it wisely. Think of the rewards when you secure that position you thrive in. Schedule time and remain proactive, never allow yourself to stay stuck in the rut.

Seeing people achieve their goals is the highlight of my role, and I would love to hear your success stories too. I want to extend a big thank you to my hundreds of clients and network contacts for being so open with their stories and their desire to encourage others. You only need one job - now is the chance to make that happen. You are career conscious and in control, now go conquer! Remember the three Ps: keep positive, productive and proactive.

This journey is like stepping stones, it may not be straightforward, and you may need to take a step sideways, before you can take a step forward. Simply readjust your plan to achieve your desired outcome. Believe that you can and you are more than halfway there. Practice being kind to your mind every day. Remember the voice that we hear in our heads has the biggest impact on us.

Final words

It has already been quite a journey and you are now on the cusp of making your dreams come true. I promised you it would be a journey where you had to work hard, challenge yourself and dig deep to recognise what you truly want.

Now you understand about "The seven steps to career consciousness", you are ready to take charge of your career and job search and you are now committed to being kind to your mind every day. I started this book by saying I never doubted that the people I've coached and supported over the years could achieve whatever it was they wanted to achieve. I said that some would call it blind faith, others believe that the power of the mind can make anything possible. Now you are in a position to take control and put the seven steps into practice.

My message has always been simple: all the hard work is not just about securing your elusive next role – it's about planning and shaping your career until the day you retire. Every month you need to be creating more achievement statements; use them in your one to ones and your appraisals and to negotiate your next pay rise! Spend some time each week or month thinking about your next move and planning the next step on your journey. This is why I am very clear about saying you will not only use this book once, but regularly to ensure you remain in control every step of the way.

May I wish you a smooth journey and remember to enjoy the ride; it is normal to feel that the journey is more of a rollercoaster ride than a merry go round. There will be highs and lows but remaining conscious means that you are completely in control. Your positive mindset will make the journey much more enjoyable.

I would like to say a huge thank you to my network for sharing their "When I grow up stories" and their interview experiences. My own career journey is made such a pleasure because of the clients and network contacts I work with; hearing the success stories and seeing careers flourish over many years. I hope you've embraced the seven steps and make your dreams come true.

If you want more positive hints and tips or career support then visit our site *www.gatewoodconsulting* follow us on twitter *@gatewoodchange*